Barrier Contraception, including: Diaphragm (contraceptive), Cervical Cap, Contraceptive Sponge, Female Condom, Silcs Diaphragm, Femcap, Today Sponge, Womb Veil

Hephaestus Books

Contents

Articles

References

Diaphragm (contraceptive)

Diaphragm (contraceptive)

Diaphragm	
1: bladder, 2: pubic bone, 3: urethra, 4: vagina, 5: uterus, 6: fornix, 7: cervix, 8: **diaphragm**, 9: rectum	
Background	
Birth control type	Barrier
First use	1880s
Failure rates (first year, with spermicide)	
Perfect use	1%%
Typical use	40-58%%
Usage	
Reversibility	Immediate
User reminders	Inserted prior intercourse with spermicide. Left in place for 6-8 hours afterwards
Clinic review	For size fitting and prescribing in some countries
Advantages and disadvantages	
STD protection	Possible
Periods	Catches menstrual flow
Benefits	May be reused 1 to 3 years
Risks	Urinary tract infection. Rare: toxic shock syndrome.

The **diaphragm** is a cervical barrier type of birth control. It is a soft latex or silicone dome with a spring molded into the rim. The spring creates a seal against the walls of the vagina.

Use

Anyone inserting or removing a diaphragm should first wash their hands, to avoid introducing harmful bacteria into the vaginal canal.

The rim of a diaphragm is squeezed into an oval or arc shape for insertion. A water-based lubricant (usually spermicide) may be applied to the rim of the diaphragm to aid insertion. One teaspoon (5mL) of spermicide may be placed in the dome of the diaphragm before insertion, or with an applicator after insertion.

The diaphragm must be inserted sometime before sexual intercourse, and remain in the vagina for 6 to 8 hours after a man's last ejaculation. For multiple acts of intercourse, it is recommended that an additional 5mL of spermicide be inserted into the vagina (not into the dome - the seal of the diaphragm should not be broken) before each act. Upon removal, a diaphragm should be cleansed with warm mild soapy water before storage. The diaphragm must be removed for cleaning at least once every 24 hours and can be re-inserted immediately.

Oil-based products should not be used with latex diaphragms. Lubricants or vaginal medications that contain oil will cause the latex to rapidly degrade and greatly increases the chances of the diaphragm breaking or tearing.

Natural latex rubber will degrade over time. Depending on usage and storage conditions, a latex diaphragm should be replaced every one to three years. Silicone diaphragms may last much longer - up to ten years.

Fitting

Diaphragms come in different sizes. A fitting appointment with a health care professional is necessary to determine which size a woman should wear.

A correctly fitting diaphragm will cover the cervix and rest snugly against the pubic bone. A diaphragm that is too small might fit inside the vagina without covering the cervix, or might become dislodged from the cervix during intercourse or bowel movements. It is also more likely, during intercourse, that a woman's partner will feel the anterior rim of a too-small diaphragm. A diaphragm that is too large will place pressure on the urethra, preventing the bladder from emptying completely and increasing the risk of urinary tract infection. A too-large diaphragm may also rub a sore on the vaginal wall.

Diaphragms should be re-fitted after a weight change of 4.5 kg (10 lb) or more. The traditional clinical guideline is that a decrease in weight may cause a woman to need a larger size, although the strength of this relationship has been questioned.

Diaphragms should also be re-fitted after any pregnancy of 14 weeks or longer. Full-term vaginal delivery especially will tend to increase the size diaphragm a woman needs, although the changes to the pelvic floor during pregnancy mean even women who experience second-trimester miscarriage, or deliver by C-section, should be refitted.

Vaginal tenting, an increase in the length of the vagina, occurs during arousal. This means that during intercourse, the diaphragm will not fit snugly against the pubic bone - it is carried higher up the vaginal canal by the movement of the cervix. If the diaphragm is inserted after arousal has begun, extra care must be taken to ensure the device is covering the cervix.

A woman might be fitted with a different size diaphragm depending on where she is in her menstrual cycle. It is common for a woman to wear a larger diaphragm during menstruation. It has been speculated that a woman may be fitted with a larger size diaphragm when she is near ovulation. The correct size for a woman is the largest size that she can wear comfortably throughout her cycle.

In the United States, diaphragms are available by prescription only. Many other countries do not require prescriptions.

Mechanism of contraception

The spring in the rim of the diaphragm forms a seal against the vaginal walls. The diaphragm covers the cervix, and physically prevents sperm from entering the uterus through the os.

Traditionally, the diaphragm has been used with spermicide, and it is widely believed the spermicide significantly increases the effectiveness of the diaphragm. Insufficient studies have been conducted to determine effectiveness without spermicide.

It is widely taught that additional spermicide must be placed in the vagina if intercourse occurs more than six hours after insertion. However, there has been very little research on how long spermicide remains active within the diaphragm. One study found that spermicidal jelly and creme used in a diaphragm retained its full spermicidal activity for twelve hours after placement of the diaphragm.

It has long been recommended that the diaphragm be left in place for at least six or eight hours after intercourse. No studies have been done to determine the validity of this recommendation, however, and some medical professionals have suggested intervals of four hours or even two hours are sufficient to ensure efficacy. Interestingly, one manufacturer of contraceptive sponges only recommends leaving the sponge in place for two hours after intercourse. However, such use of the diaphragm (removal before 6 hours post-intercourse) has never been formally studied, and cannot be recommended.

It has been suggested that diaphragms be dispensed as a one-size-fits-all device, providing all women with the most common size (70mm). However, only 33% of women fitted for a diaphragm are prescribed a 70mm size, and correct sizing of the diaphragm is widely considered necessary.

Effectiveness

The effectiveness of diaphragms, as of most forms of contraception, can be assessed two ways: *method effectiveness* and *actual effectiveness*. The method effectiveness is the proportion of couples correctly and consistently using the method who do not become pregnant. Actual effectiveness is the proportion of couples who intended that method as their sole form of birth control and do not become pregnant; it includes couples who sometimes use the method incorrectly, or sometimes not at all. Rates are generally presented for the first year of use. Most commonly the Pearl Index is used to calculate effectiveness rates, but some studies use decrement tables.

For all forms of contraception, actual effectiveness is lower than method effectiveness, due to several factors:

- mistakes on the part of those providing instructions on how to use the method
- mistakes on the part of the method's users
- conscious user non-compliance with method.

For instance, someone using a diaphragm might be fitted incorrectly by a health care provider, or by mistake remove the diaphragm too soon after intercourse, or simply choose to have intercourse without placing the diaphragm.

Contraceptive Technology reports that the method failure rate of the diaphragm with spermicide is 6% per year.

The actual pregnancy rates among diaphragm users vary depending on the population being studied, with yearly rates of 10% to 39% being reported.

Unlike some other cervical barriers, the effectiveness of the diaphragm is the same for women who have given birth as for those who have not.

Types

Diaphragms are available in diameters of 50mm to 105mm (about 2-4 inches). They are available in two different materials: latex (currently manufactured by Reflexions) and silicone (currently manufactured by Ortho, Milex and Semina). Diaphragms are also available with different types of springs in the rim.

An *arcing spring* folds into an arc shape when the sides are compressed. This is the strongest type of rim available in a diaphragm, and may be used by women with any level of vaginal tone. Unlike other spring types, arcing springs may be used by women with mild cystocele, rectocele, or retroversion. Arcing spring diaphragms may be easier to insert correctly than other spring types. Examples of arcing spring diaphragms are the Ortho All-Flex [1] and the Milex Wide-Seal Arcing [2].

A *coil spring* flattens into an oval shape when the sides are compressed. This rim is not as strong as the arcing spring, and may only be used by women with average or firm vaginal tone. If an arcing spring diaphragm is uncomfortable for a woman or, during intercourse, her partner, a coil spring may prove more satisfactory. Unlike the arcing spring diaphragms, coil springs may be inserted with a device called an introducer. Examples of coil spring diaphragms are the Ortho Coil [3], the Milex Wide-Seal Omniflex, and the Semina diaphragm [4].

A *flat spring* is much like a coil spring, but thinner. This type of rim may only be used by women with firm vaginal tone. Flat spring diaphragms may also be inserted with an introducer for women uncomfortable using their hands. Ortho used to manufacture a flat-spring diaphragm called the Ortho White. While some providers may still have Ortho White diaphragms in stock, the only current manufacturer of a flat-spring diaphragm is Reflexions.

Variations on the traditional diaphragm are being tested. The SILCS diaphragm is made of silicone, has an arcing spring, and a finger cup is molded on one end for easy removal. The Duet [5] disposable diaphragm is made of dipped polyurethane, pre-filled with BufferGel (BufferGel is currently in clinical trials as a spermicide and microbicide). Both the SILCS and Duet diaphragms are one-size-fits-all.

Advantages

The diaphragm only has to be used during intercourse. Many women, especially those who have sex less frequently, prefer barrier contraception such as the diaphragm over methods that require some action every day.

Like all cervical barriers, diaphragms may be inserted several hours before use, allowing uninterrupted foreplay and intercourse. Most couples find that neither partner can feel the diaphragm during intercourse.

The contraceptive diaphragm may be used as a menstrual device, much like the commercial product Instead. Contact with blood will discolor the diaphragm, but will not affect its contraceptive effectiveness.

The diaphragm is less expensive than many other methods of contraception.

Protection from sexually transmitted infections

There is some evidence that the cells in the cervix are particularly susceptible to certain sexually transmitted infections (STIs). Cervical barriers such as diaphragms may offer some protection against these infections. However, research conducted to test whether the diaphragm offers protection from HIV found that women provided with both male condoms and a diaphragm experienced the same rate of HIV infection as women provided with male condoms alone.

Because pelvic inflammatory disease (PID) is caused by certain STIs, diaphragms may lower the risk of PID. Cervical barriers may also protect against human papillomavirus (HPV), the virus that causes cervical cancer, although the protection appears to be due to the spermicide used with diaphragms and not the barrier itself.

Diaphragms are also considered a good candidate as a delivery method for microbicides (preparations that, used vaginally, protect against STIs) that are currently in development.

Risks

Women (or their partners) who are allergic to latex should not use a latex diaphragm.

Diaphragms are associated with an increased risk of urinary tract infection (UTI) Urinating before inserting the diaphragm, and also after intercourse, may reduce this risk.

Toxic shock syndrome (TSS) occurs at a rate of 2.4 cases per 100,000 women using diaphragms, almost exclusively when the device is left in place longer than 24 hours.

The increase in risk of UTI's may be due to the diaphragm applying pressure to the urethra, especially if the diaphragm is too large, and causing irritation and preventing the bladder from emptying fully. However, the spermicide nonoxynol-9 is itself associated with increased risk of UTI, yeast infection, and bacterial vaginosis. For this reason, some advocate use of lactic acid or lemon juice based spermicides, which might have fewer side effects. Although these alternative spermicides have been shown to immobilize sperm in the laboratory, their effect on pregnancy rates in humans has never been studied.

It has also been suggested that, for women who experience side effects from nonoxynol-9, it may be acceptable to use the diaphragm without any spermicide. One study found an actual pregnancy rate of 24% per year in women using the diaphragm without spermicide; however, all women in this study were given a 60mm diaphragm rather than being fitted by a clinician. Other studies have been small and given conflicting results. The current recommendation is still for all diaphragm users to use spermicide with the device.

History

The idea of blocking the cervix to prevent pregnancy is thousands of years old. Various cultures have used cervix-shaped devices such as oiled paper cones or lemon halves, or have made sticky mixtures that include honey or cedar rosin to be applied to the cervical opening. However, the diaphragm - which stays in place because of the spring in its rim, rather than hooking over the cervix or being sticky - is of much more recent origin.

An important precursor to the invention of the diaphragm was the rubber vulcanization process, patented by Charles Goodyear in 1844. In the 1880s, a German gynecologist C. Haase published the first description of a rubber contraceptive device with a spring molded into the rim. Haase wrote under the pseudonym Wilhelm P.J. Mensinga, and the Mensinga diaphragm was the only brand available for many decades. In the United States, the physician Edward Bliss Foote designed and sold an early form of occlusive pessary under the name "womb veil" starting in the 1860s.

American birth control activist Margaret Sanger fled to Europe in 1914 to escape prosecution under the Comstock laws, which prohibited sending contraceptive devices, or information about contraception, through the mail. Sanger learned about the diaphragm in the Netherlands and introduced the product to the United States when she returned in 1916. Sanger and her second husband, Noah Slee, illegally imported large quantities of the devices from Germany and the Netherlands. In 1925, Slee provided funding to Sanger's friend Herbert Simonds, who used the funds to found the first diaphragm manufacturing company in the U.S., the Holland-Rantos Company.

Diaphragms played a role in overturning the federal Comstock Act. In 1932, Sanger arranged for a Japanese manufacturer to mail a package of diaphragms to a New York physician who supported Sanger's activism. U.S. customs confiscated the package, and Sanger helped file a lawsuit. In 1936, in the court case *United States v. One Package of Japanese Pessaries*, a federal appellate court ruled that the package could be delivered.

Although in Europe, the cervical cap was more popular than the diaphragm, the diaphragm became one of the most widely used contraceptives in the United States. In 1940, one-third of all U.S. married couples used a diaphragm for contraception. The number of women using diaphragms dropped dramatically after the 1960s introduction of the IUD and the combined oral contraceptive pill. In 1965, only 10% of U.S. married couples used a diaphragm for contraception. That number has continued to fall, and in 2002 only 0.2% of American women were using a diaphragm as their primary method of contraception.

External links

- Cervical Barrier Advancement Society [6]
- DiaphragmsAndCaps [7] Yahoo! group "*For women using or considering a barrier*"

Further reading

- Halberstam, David (1994). *The Fifties*. New York: Fawcett Columbine.
- McCann, Carole R. (1994). *Birth Control Politics in the United States, 1916–1945*. Ithaca: Cornell University Press.
- Tobin, Kathleen (2001). *The American Religious Debate Over Birth Control, 1907–1937*. Jefferson: McFarland & Company.

Cervical cap

Cervical cap

Cervical cap	
Oves brand cervical cap (discontinued)	
Background	
Birth control type	Barrier
First use	1838
Pregnancy rates (first year)	
Perfect use	Prentif, nulliparous:9% Prentif, parous:26%
Typical use	Prentif, nulliparous:16% Prentif, parous:32% Lea's Shield: 15%
Usage	
Reversibility	Immediate
User reminders	Inserted with spermicide and left in place for 6 hours after intercourse
Clinic review	For fitting and subsequent replacements
Advantages and disadvantages	
Benefits	Femcap may be left in place for 48 hours

The **cervical cap** is a form of barrier contraception. A cervical cap fits over the cervix and blocks sperm from entering the uterus through the external orifice of the uterus, called the *os*. As of February 2009, the FemCap was the only type of cervical cap available in the United States.

Terminology

The term *cervical cap* has been used to refer to a number of barrier contraceptives, including the Prentif, Dumas, Vimule, and Oves devices. In the United States, Prentif was the only brand available for several decades (Prentif was withdrawn from the U.S. market in 2005). During this time, it was common to use the term *cervical cap* to refer exclusively to the Prentif brand.

The Lea's Shield was a cervical barrier device which was discontinued as of 2008. Some sources use *cervical cap* to refer to the FemCap and Lea's Shield. Other sources include FemCap in the term *cervical cap*, but classified the Lea's Shield as a distinct device.

Cervical caps or conception caps have also been designed as a form of assisted reproductive technology, used to help people experiencing infertility.

History

Ancient

The idea of blocking the cervix to prevent pregnancy is thousands of years old. Various cultures have used cervix-shaped devices such as oiled paper cones or lemon halves. Others made sticky mixtures that included honey or cedar rosin, to be applied to the os. The modern idea of a cervical cap as a fitted device that seals itself against the vaginal walls is of more recent origin; it emerged within the past century.

1800s

In 1838, German gynecologist Friedrich Wilde created the first modern cervical cap by making custom-made rubber molds of the cervix for some of his patients. These caps were probably short-lived, as uncured rubber degrades fairly quickly. An important precursor to the invention of more lasting caps was the rubber vulcanization process, patented by Charles Goodyear in 1844. An occlusive pessary marketed in the United States as the "womb veil" seems to have been an early form of diaphragm or cervical cap.

Over the next several decades, the cervical cap became the most widely used barrier contraceptive method in Western Europe and England. Although the diaphragm was always more popular in the United States than the cervical cap, the cap was also common.

1900s

Many designs were developed in the later 19th and early 20th century. The Vimule cap became available as early as 1927. A book by Vimule and Co., published in 1898, advertises the Vimule Cap. The Prentif brand cap was introduced in the early 1930s. The Dumas cap was initially made of plastic, and was available by the 1940s. Lamberts (Dalston) Ltd. of the UK manufactured these three cap types.

Other types of caps had stems to hold them in place in the cervix; some of the stems actually extended into the uterus. These stem pessaries became precursors to the modern intrauterine device.

Use of all barrier methods, but especially cervical barriers, dropped dramatically after the 1960s introduction of the combined oral contraceptive pill and the intrauterine device. In 1976, the U.S. government enacted the Medical Device Amendment. This law required all manufacturers of medical devices to provide the United States Food and Drug Administration (FDA) with data on the safety and efficacy of those devices. Lamberts (Dalston) Ltd., the only manufacturer at that time, failed to provide this information, and the FDA banned the use of cervical caps in the United States.

In the late 1970s, the FDA reclassified the cervical cap as an investigational device, and it regained limited availability. Within a few years, the FDA withdrew investigational status from the Vimule cap, following a study that associated its use with vaginal lacerations. In 1988, the Prentif cap gained FDA approval. The feminist movement played a large role in re-introducing the cervical cap to the United States. One paper called its involvement at all steps of the FDA approval process "unprecedented."

Types

Several brands of caps were manufactured during the late 20th century and early 21st century. They can be divided into two types: cavity rim caps, and other caps. Cavity rim caps adhere to the cervix, while other caps adhere to the vaginal walls around the cervix.

The cavity rim caps are Prentif, made of latex, and the disposable cap Oves, made of silicone. There are three sizes of Prentif: 22, 25, 28, and 31 mm. There are three sizes of Oves: 26, 28, and 30 mm. Unique among cervical caps, it adheres to the cervix by surface tension, rather than by suction.

The other devices are the latex Dumas and Vimule, and the silicone FemCap, Lea's Shield, and Shanghai Lily. There are five sizes of Dumas: 50, 55, 60, 65, and 75 mm. There are three sizes of Vimule: 42, 48, and 52 mm. There are three sizes of FemCap: 22, 26, and 30 mm. There are four sizes of Shanghai Lily: 54, 58, 62, and 66 mm. Lea's Shield is manufactured in a single size. Unlike the other caps, Lea's Shield has a one-way air valve that helps it seal to the vaginal walls. The valve also allows the passage of cervical mucus. FemCap does not have such a valve and as such can be used to collect cervical mucus to support the billings method Both Lea's Shield and FemCap have loops to assist in removal.

Shanghai Lily is only available in China. As of 2008, many of the other devices are no longer being manufactured: Prentif, Vimule, and Dumas have been discontinued. Oves is only being sold as a *conception cap*, not as a birth control device. As of February 2009, FemCap was the only brand of cervical cap available in the United States. FemCap is also available in the UK via the NHS on prescription and is often distributed free from Family Planning Clinics depending on the health authority. Lea's Shield is only available as the German brand LEA contraceptivum.

Fitting

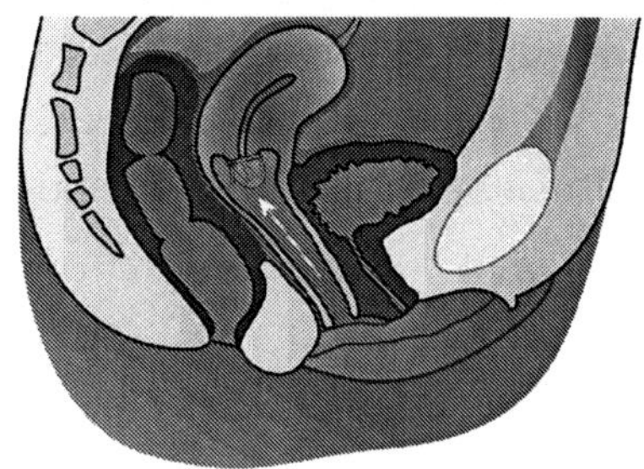
Position of a cavity rim cap

Individuals who wish to use a cervical cap are screened by a health care provider to determine if a cervical cap, or one brand of cap, is appropriate for them. If a cap is determined to be appropriate, the provider will determine the proper size. The user must be refitted after any duration of pregnancy, whether the pregnancy is aborted, miscarried, or carried to term through vaginal childbirth or caesarean section.

Several factors may make a cap inappropriate for a particular woman. Women who have given birth may have scar tissue or irregularly shaped cervixes that interfere with the cap forming a good seal. For some women, available sizes of cervical caps do not provide a correct fit. Also, cavity rim caps are not recommended for women with an anteflexed uterus.

Obtaining a fitting appointment may be difficult for some women. A 1997 survey in the United States found that most family medicine residents had no experience with prescription methods of birth control other than oral contraceptives. In some countries, some devices (such as the Lea's Shield) are available without a prescription.

Use

The first step in inserting or removing a cervical cap is handwashing, to avoid introducing harmful bacteria into the vaginal canal. The cap is inserted prior to sexual intercourse; some sources state that insertion prior to sexual arousal decreases the risk of incorrect placement. Most sources recommend the use of spermicide with the cap, but some sources say spermicide use is optional.

The cap remains in the vagina for a minimum of 6 or 8 hours after the last intravaginal ejaculation. It is recommended the cap be removed within 72 hours (within 48 hours recommended in the U.S.) Other than the disposable Oves cap, after use cervical caps are washed and stored for reuse. Silicone devices may be boiled to sterilize them. Reusable caps may last for one or two years.

Effectiveness

The effectiveness of cervical caps, as of most forms of contraception, can be assessed two ways: *method effectiveness* and *actual effectiveness*. The method effectiveness is the proportion of couples correctly and consistently using the method who do not become pregnant. Actual effectiveness is the proportion of couples who intended that method as their sole form of birth control and do not become pregnant; it includes couples who sometimes use the method incorrectly, or sometimes not at all. Rates are generally presented for the first year of use. Most commonly the Pearl Index is used to calculate effectiveness rates, but some studies use decrement tables.

Contraceptive Technology reports that the method failure rate of the Prentif cervical cap with spermicide is 9% per year for nulliparous women (women who have never given birth), and 26% per year for parous women. The actual pregnancy rates among Prentif users vary depending on the population being studied, with yearly rates of 11% to 32% being reported.

Little data is available on the effectiveness of the Oves cap and Femcap. The Oves manufacturer cites one small study of 17 users. The Femcap website does not cite any data on the current version of the Femcap; but lists data for an older version which is no longer approved by the FDA.

The only effectiveness trial of Lea's Shield was too small to determine method effectiveness. The actual pregnancy rate was 15% per year. Of the women in the trial, 85% were parous (had given birth). The study authors estimate that for nulliparous women (those who have never given birth) the pregnancy rate in typical use may be lower, around 5% per year.

Acceptability

The Oves cap and the new version of the Femcap performed poorly in user acceptability studies. The study on the Femcap concluded that the modifications to the FemCap significantly increased pain and discomfort among female users and their male sex partners, and that the modifications decreased acceptability of the device compared with the earlier version. The study of the Oves cap reported that few women indicated that they would use the cap in the future.

A pilot study conducted in Britain prior to the Lea's Shield's approval concluded that the Lea's Shield "may be acceptable to a highly select minority of women".

As of 2002, the cervical cap was one of the least common methods of contraception in the United States. A 2002 study indicated that of sexually active American women, 0.6% are currently using either the cervical cap, contraceptive sponge, or female condom as their primary method of contraception, and fewer than 1% have ever used a cervical cap.

External links

- Cervical Barrier Advancement Society [6]
- Diaphragms and Caps [1] (Yahoo Group)
- Femcap [2] website
- Oves [3] website

Barrier contraception

Barrier contraception

Barrier contraception	
Background	
Birth control type	Barrier
First use	Plastic & silicone (1900s) Rubber/latex (1800s) Other materials (Ancient)
Failure rates (first year)	
Perfect use	method dependent%
Typical use	method dependent%
Usage	
User reminders	Must be applied prior to intercourse.
Clinic review	Size assessment for some methods
Advantages and disadvantages	
STD protection	Method dependent
Weight gain	No
Benefits	No external drugs taken

Barrier contraception methods prevent pregnancy by physically preventing sperm from entering the uterus.

History

The earliest recorded barrier methods are those of stem pessaries, found in Egypt. The diaphragm and reusable condoms became common after the invention of rubber vulcanization in the early nineteenth century. Condoms became even more popular after the 1930s invention of latex, which enabled the creation of thinner, disposable prophylactics.

Methods

The following are barrier methods of contraception.

- Condom
- Female condom
- Cervical cap (including Lea's Shield)
- Diaphragm
- SILCS diaphragm (still in clinical testing)

The contraceptive sponge is usually considered a barrier method, but not always, as its effectiveness relies largely on spermicide.

The male condom provides excellent protection against sexually transmitted infections. Using a condom is sometimes referred to as "practicing safer sex".

Related

- Dental dams have no contraceptive use, but offer STD protection during oral sex (see unprotected sex).

Contraceptive sponge

Contraceptive sponge

Contraceptive sponge	
Protectaid sponge, in its plastic tray. It is removed from the tray before use.	
Background	
Birth control type	Barrier
First use	1983
Failure rates (first year)	
Perfect use	Nulliparous:9% Parous:26%
Typical use	Nulliparous:16% Parous:32%
Usage	
Reversibility	Immediate
User reminders	?
Advantages and disadvantages	
STD protection	No
Benefits	May be inserted 12–24 hours before intercourse.
Risks	yeast infection, rarely toxic shock syndrome

The **contraceptive sponge** combines barrier and spermicidal methods to prevent conception. Three brands are marketed: Pharmatex, Protectaid and Today. Pharmatex is marketed in France and Quebec; Protectaid in Canada and Europe; and Today in the United States. For a while, the Today brand was not being manufactured. In mid May 2009, Mayer Laboratories, Inc.[1], the distributor of the Today Vaginal Contraceptive Sponge [2] for the US, Canada and the EU, announced the Today Sponge had been re-launched in the United States.

The sponges are inserted vaginally prior to intercourse and must be placed over the cervix to be effective. To facilitate removal, Today has an elastic band across the sponge; Protectaid has two slots.

Sponges provide no protection from sexually transmitted infections (STIs).

Effectiveness

The manufacturer of the Today sponge reports effectiveness for prevention of pregnancy of 89% to 91% when used correctly and consistently. When packaging directions are not followed for every act of intercourse, effectiveness rates of 84% to 89% are reported. Other sources cite poorer effectiveness rates for women who have given birth - 74% during correct and consistent use, and 68% during typical use.

Studies of Protectaid have found effectiveness rates of 77% to 91%.

Studies of Pharmatex have found perfect use effectiveness rates of over 99% per year. Typical use of Pharmatex results in effectiveness of 81% per year. Sponges may be used in conjunction with another method of birth control such as condoms to increase effectiveness.

Use

The Today sponge must run under water until thoroughly wet before insertion. The Protectaid and Pharmatex sponges come ready to use.

The sponge can be inserted up to 24 hours before intercourse. It must be left in place for at least six hours after the last time you have intercourse. It should not be worn for more than 30 hours in a row.[3]

History

The Today Sponge was introduced in the United States in 1983. The Pharmatex sponge was introduced in France and the Quebec province in Canada in 1984. The Protectaid sponge was introduced in Canada in 1996, and in Europe in 2000. All three brands are available outside their normal marketing areas through internet retailers.

The Today sponge actually dates back to 1976 when it was created by Bruce Ward Vorhauer. Vorhauer struggled for 7 years to get the device approved and on the market. Personal money problems forced Vorhauer to sell the entire manufacturing operation to American Home Products, now Wyeth. Almost the entire content of the facility was moved to the Whitehall-Robbins facility in Hammonton, NJ from its original California home. The sponge was removed from the U.S. market in 1994 after problems were found at the facility related to the DI water system. The water system, which was originally sized for much larger production, could not produce the small amounts of DI water required for this one product and became repeatedly contaminated. Wyeth stopped selling the sponge rather than move production or modify its plant, based on slumping sales and to avoid any further FDA issues.

In 1998, Allendale Pharmaceuticals bought the patents and the complex manufacturing equipment. New FDA standards for manufacturing and record-keeping forced repeated delays (some users started calling it the "Real soon now sponge"), but the Today sponge was finally re-introduced in Canada in March 2003, and in the U.S. in September 2005. In January 2007, Allendale Pharmaceuticals was acquired by Synova Healthcare, Inc. In December 2007 Synova filed for bankruptcy reorganization; in 2008 the manufacturing rights to the Today sponge were purchased by Alvogen. As of 2008, the Today Sponge was not being manufactured. In mid May 2009, Mayer Laboratories, Inc.[1], the distributor of the Today Vaginal Contraceptive Sponge [2] for the US, Canada and the EU, announced the Today Sponge had been re-launched in the United States.

Spermicide

Sponges are a physical barrier, trapping sperm and preventing their passage through the cervix into the female reproductive system. The spermicide is an important component of pregnancy prevention; each brand offers a different formula.

The Today sponge contains 1,000 milligrams (mg) of nonoxynol-9. Protectaid contains 5,000 mg of the F-5 gel, with three active ingredients (6.25 mg of nonoxynol-9, 6.25 mg of benzalkonium chloride, and 25 mg of sodium cholate). Pharmatex contains 60 mg of benzalkonium chloride.

Side effects

Some people are allergic to the spermicide used in the sponge. Women who use contraceptive sponges have an increased risk of yeast infection and urinary tract infection. Improper use, such as leaving the sponge in too long, can result in toxic shock syndrome.

In popular culture

- Shortly after they were taken off the U.S. market, the sponge was featured in an episode of the sitcom *Seinfeld* titled "The Sponge". In the episode, the character Elaine Benes conserves her remaining contraceptive sponges by refusing intercourse unless she is certain her partner is "sponge worthy".
- The film *Clueless* features a scene where the characters Dionne and Tai are discussing sex and Dionne is heard to ask Tai if the sponge would still work if the user has sex in water.

External links

- Contraceptive Sponge [4] - American Pregnancy Association
- Contraceptive Sponge [5] - CoolNurse.com
- Spongeworthiness [6] - Salon.com
- The Contraceptive Sponge [7] - DrDonnica.com
- Contraceptive Sponges (Today / Protectaid / Pharmatex) [8] - FAQ thread on Ovusoft.com message boards

Female condom

Female condom

Female condom	
Polyurethane female condom	
Background	
Birth control type	Barrier
First use	1980s
Failure rates (first year)	
Perfect use	5%
Typical use	21%
Usage	
Reversibility	Immediate
User reminders	?
Advantages and disadvantages	
STD protection	Yes
Benefits	No external drugs or clinic visits required

A **female condom** is a device that is used during sexual intercourse as a barrier contraceptive and to reduce the risk of sexually transmitted infections (STIs—such as gonorrhea, syphilis, and HIV). Invented by Danish MD Lasse Hessel, it is worn internally by the receptive partner and physically blocks ejaculated semen from entering that person's body. Female condoms can be used by the receptive partner during anal sex.

The female condom is a pouch with flexible rings at each end. Before vaginal intercourse, the ring inside the pouch is inserted deep into the vagina, holding the condom in the vagina. The penis is directed into the pouch through the ring at the open end, which stays outside the vaginal opening during intercourse.

Versions and materials

The female condom was first made from polyurethane. This version is officially called the "FC Female Condom". A newer version is made of nitrile rubber and called "FC2" (this material change was announced in September 2005). The newer nitrile condoms are less likely to make potentially distracting crinkling noises. It is hoped the nitrile condoms will also allow for significant reductions in female condom pricing. This line of condoms is manufactured by The Female Health Company, USA. FC1 and FC2 are the only female condoms encouraged by the World Health Organization (WHO) as an additional tool for protecting sexual and reproductive health. The UNFPA (a U.N. agency) has incorporated the female condom into national programming. They are sold under many brand names, including *Reality, Femidom, Dominique, Femy, Myfemy, Protectiv* and *Care*.

A recent version of the female condom is made from natural latex, the same material used in male condoms. This condom does not make the noises some experience with plastic condoms. This type of female condom is manufactured by Medtech Products Ltd, India. It is sold under various brand names, including *Reddy*, *V Amour*, *L'amour*, *VA WOW Feminine condom*, and *Sutra*. One more clinical trial is required before it can be considered for FDA approval in the United States.

The global health nonprofit Program for Appropriate Technology in Health (PATH) has also developed a female condom tailored for use in developing countries. The Woman's Condom is manufactured by Shanghai Dahua Medical Apparatus in China and is currently undergoing clinical trials.

Costs and "reuse" of the (polyurethane) original FC

The per unit price of female condoms is higher than male condoms but there is some evidence to suggest that polyurethane female condoms can be washed, disinfected, and reused.

Re-using the polyurethane female condom is not considered as safe as using a new one, however the WHO says, "Batches of new, unused female condoms were subjected to seven cycles of disinfection, washing, drying and re-lubrication, reflecting the steps and procedures in the draft protocol, but at considerably higher concentrations of bleach and for longer durations. All female condom batches met the manufacturing quality assessment specifications for structural integrity after the test cycles. ... Disinfection, washing, drying, re-lubrication and reuse of the device were not associated with penile discharge, symptomatic vaginal irritation or adverse colposcopic findings in study volunteers." A presentation at the 1998 International AIDS conference concluded that "washing, drying and re-lubricating the female condom up to ten times does not significantly alter the structural integrity of the device. Further microbiological and virological tests are required before re-use of the female condom can be recommended."

Lubrication

Advantages

The plastic female condoms have the advantage of being compatible with oil-based lubricants as they are not made of latex. The external genitals of the wearer and the base of the penis of the inserting partner may be more protected than when the male condom is used, however see studies below. Inserting a female condom does not require male erection.

Worldwide use

Sales of female condoms have been disappointing in developed countries, though developing countries are increasingly using them to complement already existing family planning and HIV/AIDS programming. Probable causes for poor sales are that inserting the female condom is a skill that has to be learned and that female condoms can be significantly more expensive than male condoms (upwards of 2 or 3 times the cost). Also, reported "rustling" sounds during intercourse turn off some potential users, as does the visibility of the outer ring which remains outside the vagina.

In November 2005, the World YWCA called on national health ministries and international donors to commit to purchasing 180 million female condoms for global distribution in 2006, stating that "Female condoms remain the only tool for HIV prevention that women can initiate and control," but that they remain virtually inaccessible to women in the developing world due to their high cost of 72¢ per piece. If 180 million female condoms were ordered, the price of a single female condom was projected to decline to 22¢.

In 2005, 12 million female condoms were distributed to women in the developing world. By comparison, between 6 and 9 billion male condoms were distributed that year.

Similar prophylactics that may not be available

- The Barrier
  - **Coverage / How it is held in place:** It fits over the vulva and perineum and is held in place with thick elastic straps that encircle the women's upper legs. The tube-shaped pouch is about 1½ times larger and 2 times thicker than a male condom. The penis never directly touches the woman's outer or inner genitalia
  - **Material:** latex
- The Bikini Condom
  - **Coverage / How it is held in place:** "looks like a G-string panty"
  - **Effectiveness:** thicker and less slippage than male condoms, a breakage rate of 0.5%, compared to 1–2% for male condoms

- **Advantages:** condom pouch can be automatically introduced into the vagina with coitus, reported heightened sensation for women
- **Cost—reuse:** "can be used 5–10 times"

- Women's Choice Female Condom
    - **Coverage / How it is held in place:** Has a 2-inch-diameter (51 mm) flexible ring that covers the introitus, and a thickened dome of latex resembling a diaphragm at the deep end
    - **Pre-lubrication / Spermicide:** silicone lubrication

External links

- Detailed Guide to use Female Condom [1] How to use and take out safely a female condom
- Prevention Now! Expanding Global Access to Female Condoms [2]
- "Female Condoms: Sexual Freedom Doesn't Come Free" posted on Alternet [5]
- "Whatever happened to the Femidom?" in *Guardian* [6]
- PATH's woman's condom [7]
- How to put on a female condom [8] An illustrated guide from Canadian health experts
- Planned Parenthood [9] Female Condom

SILCS diaphragm

SILCS diaphragm

Main article: diaphragm (contraceptive)

The **SILCS diaphragm** is a silicone barrier contraceptive device which is inserted vaginally to cover the cervix. The SILCS device was developed by the Program for Appropriate Technology in Health (PATH) and SILCS, Inc. USAID-supported *Contraceptive Research and Development Program* (CONRAD) supported product development and clinical trials.

It functions identically to a normal contraceptive diaphragm, but avoids the need for many sizes and a pelvic exam for a correct fit; it is designed as a "one size fits most" device.

The designers of the device relied heavily on results from studies of current and former diaphragm users and clinicians to improve acceptability and satisfaction. Women are evaluating the new device for comfort and ease-of-use in studies, underway in the Dominican Republic, South Africa, Thailand, and the United States.

External links

- SILCS diaphragm [1], by PATH

FemCap

FemCap	
Background	
Birth control type	Barrier
First use	?
pregnancy rates (first year)	
Perfect use	no data%
Typical use	estimated at 7.6%
Usage	
Reversibility	Immediate
User reminders	Inserted with spermicide and left in place for 6 hours after intercourse
Clinic review	For fitting and subsequent replacements
Advantages and disadvantages	
Benefits	May be left in place for 48 hours

FemCap is a cervical barrier contraceptive. As of February 2009, FemCap is the only brand of cervical cap available in the United States.

FemCap is made of silicone, its shape is similar to a sailor's hat. FemCap has had two designs; the newer design added a loop, molded into the silicone, to assist with removal of the device. Only the newer design is available. There are three sizes of FemCap: 22, 26, and 30 mm. The smallest rim diameter (22mm) is intended for women who have never been pregnant. The medium (26mm) cap is intended for women who have been pregnant but have not had a vaginal delivery. The largest (30mm) is intended for women who have had a vaginal delivery of a full-term baby. The only exception to this rule, if a woman had a spontaneous miscarriage and/or she was not aware of it, in which case she should receive the 26mm FemCap. If the woman and her doctor are in doubt it is more appropriate to use the 26mm FemCap.

The new version of the Femcap performed poorly in a user acceptability study, suggesting that the modifications to the FemCap significantly increased coital pain or discomfort among female users and their male sex partners, and that the modifications did not improve ease of use overall. However,

FemCap users are still less likely to report such pain or discomfort than diaphragm users.

See also

- Cervical cap
- Barrier contraception

References

Sources

- FemCap: Clinician Protocol [1], states effectiveness rate listed in infobox.

External links

- FemCap [2], official site
- FDA information on FemCap [2]

Today sponge

Today sponge

The Today Sponge is a barrier contraceptive made of polyurethane foam that contains the spermicide, nonoxynol 9, to provide contraceptive protection. The Today Sponge is sold over the counter at large retail stores in the U.S and online. Other brands of contraceptive sponges include Pharmatex and Protectaid. Originally launched in 1983, over 150 million sponges have been sold and more than 3 million women have used it. The Today Sponge does not provide protection against sexually transmitted diseases (STD's).

Today Sponge creates a physical barrier between the sperm and the cervix. The Today Sponge is inserted through the vagina and must be placed up against the cervix to be effective. The Today Sponge provides contraceptive protection by blocking sperm from entering the cervix, absorbing sperm, and releasing the spermicide, nonoxynol 9 to kill sperm. Today Sponge protects for 24 hours even through multiple acts of intercourse.

Benefits and Drawbacks

Benefits • Hormone-free • Safe and effective • Available over the counter (non prescription) • 24 hour protection • Allows spontaneity without re-application • Effective immediately upon insertion • Can be used only when needed it • Not messy

Drawbacks • Does not protect against sexually transmitted diseases • Reports of sensitivity and allergies to nonoxynol 9 • Reduced effectiveness when not used consistently and correctly • Requires water for application • Rare cases of Toxic Shock Syndrome (TSS) have been reported in women using barrier contraceptives, including the sponge.

Use

The Today Sponge comes wrapped in air-tight plastic. Prior to insertion, the Today Sponge must be wet thoroughly with clean water and made sudsy. Using your fingers, the Today Sponge is then moved deep into the vagina and placed up against the cervix. Women who are comfortable wearing tampons find it easier to use. Intercourse can commence immediately after insertion. The Today Sponge protects against pregnancy for up to 24 hours. Before removal, the Today Sponge must be left in place for at least six hours after the last act of intercourse. The Today Sponge comes with a band to facilitate removal. Today Sponge should not be left inside the vagina for more than 30 hours.

Active Ingredient

Nonoxynol 9 (1000 mg)

Inactive Ingredients

Benzoic acid, citric acid, sodium dihydrogen citrate, sodium metabisulfite, sorbic acid water in a polyurethane foam sponge.

Effectiveness

In a worldwide trial published in 1985, 9-11% of women became pregnant during the first year of use when the product was used correctly all the time. The pregnancy rate increased to 13-16% when the product was not used correctly or consistently for every act of intercourse.

Other Studies on Effectiveness

In 1979 international clinical trials began to evaluate the effectiveness, side effects, and user acceptability of the Today Sponge. The international studies took place at 20 clinics, and consisted of 1847 women. Five hundred seventy-nine women between the ages of 18-40 completed the 12 month study. Pregnancies during this time were classified as user failures (pregnancies that occurred because the woman did not use the sponge in the manner described), and method failures (pregnancies that occurred even though the sponge was consistently used correctly. In the 0-12 month period the worldwide method effectiveness rate was 89.9% (10.1 per 100 women). However, at the second year, the method effectiveness rate for the subset of US clinics was 96.6% (3.4 per 100 women). The causes for the variation was not identified ..

Side Effects and Warnings

Some people are sensitive or allergic to nonoxynol 9, the spermicide used in the Today Sponge. Although rare, Toxic Shock Syndrome has been reported and can occur especially with improper use of the Today Sponge. The Today Sponge does not protect against sexually transmitted diseases (STD's).

On TV

The Today Sponge is well recognized for its appearance in an episode of the sitcom Seinfeld titled "The Sponge". In the episode, the character Elaine Benes stocks up on sponges because they are being discontinued. Elaine then becomes very selective with her sexual partners and refuses intercourse unless she determines her partner to be "sponge worthy".

History

2009 - Today Sponge is re-launched in more than 13,000 drug stores across the United States and on-line; In its initial launch Today Sponge was available at 6,500 CVS/Longs drug stores in May and in 6,700 Walgreens and 200 Duane Reade locations in June.

2007 - Synova Healthcare, Inc, acquires Allendale Pharmaceuticals. 11 months later Synova files for bankruptcy. Alvogen Group, Inc. purchases rights to the Today Sponge and, in late 2008, assigns distribution rights to Mayer Labs.

2005 - The Today Sponge is re-introduced in Canada in March 2003 and in the U.S. in September 2005. Allendale Pharmaceuticals purchased the patents and the complex manufacturing equipment in 1998 to produce the Today Sponge. New FDA standards force repeated delays.

1994 - The Today Sponge is removed from the U.S market due to factory compliance issues. Rather than update the plant to meet requirements, Wyeth Pharmaceuticals stopped selling the sponge.

1983 - The Today Sponge is introduced in the United States and quickly becomes the most popular OTC female contraceptive in North America8.

Womb veil

Womb veil

The **womb veil** was a 19th-century American form of barrier contraception consisting of an occlusive pessary made of rubber. It was the forerunner to the modern diaphragm and cervical cap. The name was first used by Edward Bliss Foote in 1863 for the device he designed and marketed. "Womb veil" became the most common 19th-century American term for similar devices, and continued to be used into the early 20th century. Womb veils were among a "range of contraceptive technology of questionable efficacy" available to American women of the 1800s, forms of which began to be advertised in the 1830s and 1840s. They could be bought widely through mail-order catalogues; when induced abortion was criminalized in the United States during the 1870s, reliance on birth control increased. Womb veils were touted as a discreet form of contraception, with one catalogue of erotic products from the 1860s promising that they could be "used by the female without danger of detection by the male."

The use of rubber pessaries for contraception likely arose from the 19th-century practice of correcting a prolapsed uterus with such a device; the condition seems to have been far more frequently diagnosed than its incidence would warrant, and at times may have been a fiction for employing a pessary for birth control. As with the production of condoms for men, the development of vulcanized rubber by Charles Goodyear helped make barrier contraceptives for women more reliable and inexpensive. Other terms for the contraceptive diaphragm were "female preventatives", "female protectors", "Victoria's protectors", and the "French pessary" ("F.P.") or "pessaire preventif". This linguistic variety, some of it euphemistic, makes it difficult to distinguish in the literature among diaphragms, cervical caps, female condoms, and other pessaries; one form of "womb veil" is described in 1890 as "like a ring pessary covered by a membraneous envelope." Another source in 1895 describes it as "a small soft rubber cup surrounded at the brim by a flexible rubber ring about an inch or inch and a quarter in diameter."

Social history

The Popular Health Movement of the Jacksonian era encouraged the sharing of knowledge about contraception, and contraceptive devices were advertised openly in newspaper ads and in brochures throughout the first half of the 19th century. Among their proponents was the physician Edward Bliss Foote. Foote introduced his device, the womb veil, in a self-published book entitled *Medical Common Sense*:

> This consists of an India-rubber contrivance which the female easily adjusts in the vagina *before* copulation, and which spreads a thin tissue of rubber before the mouth of the womb so as to prevent the seminal aura from entering. ... Conception cannot possibly take place when it is used. The full enjoyment of the conjugal embrace can be indulged in during coition. The husband would hardly be likely to know that it was being used, unless told by the wife. ... It places conception entirely under the control of the wife, to whom it naturally belongs; for it is for her to say at what time and under what circumstances, she will become the mother, and the moral, religious, and physical instructress of offpsring.

Foote appears to have been the first to use the term "womb veil", in introducing his vaginal diaphragm in 1863. The explicitness of his description is regarded as "rather remarkable" for its time. Foote touted his device as "the only reliable means yet discovered for the prevention of conception," and sold it "closely sealed" through the mail at a cost of $6. Foote may have gotten the idea for his device from an 1838 German treatise on cervical caps, or from acquaintance with the German tradition of midwifery that had been brought to the United States. Although he mentions his intention to obtain a patent, none is recorded.

Emma Goldman was among those who promoted the use of "womb veils" as contraception

"Succinct, straightforward" advertising for birth control devices, as well as for aphrodisiacs and drugs to induce abortion and cure venereal disease, had been common in newspapers of the 1830s and 40s. But in 1873, the Comstock laws made it illegal to disseminate information about contraception. The following year, Foote was arrested and convicted under Comstock. His pamphlets were seized and destroyed, although his descriptions of the womb veil survive in early editions of his book. In subsequent editions, he was required to cut back the section on contraception to focus on douching, usually referred to in the literature of the time as the use of syringes. Retailers were subjected to raids, with womb veils among the contraceptive devices confiscated. Although contraceptive information in popular media was curtailed, technical and medical journals and textbooks were not subject to this regulation, and physicians continued to discuss both issues and technologies pertaining to birth control.

The early 20th century saw a resurgence of interest in birth control in the United States, due largely to the efforts of Margaret Sanger and other social activists. One of the most outspoken advocates for contraception during this time was Emma Goldman, who openly defied the Comstock laws by recommending the womb veil in leaflets she distributed after her lectures.

Efficacy and side effects

The womb veil, described in medical Latin as a type of *pessarium occlusivum*, was considered by some medical authorities to be effective if fitted and inserted correctly. Post-coital douching was often recommended in conjunction with its use. Prolonged use of the device was reported on occasion to produce side effects, some of which pointed toward a need for better hygiene. Serious ulcerations were reported among those who wore it too long or without proper care. In a report to the New Haven Medical Association, one doctor blamed the womb veil for a woman's nocturnal seizures. A gynecologist noted that the rubber womb veil might cause irritation or itching, but reckoned that the "opportunity for increased or unlimited intercourse" was the proximate cause. Another physician who promoted contraception as a way to avoid resorting to abortion found that some users had been disappointed in the womb veil; he recommended douching as a more effective means.

One physican found the womb veil to be "harmless" and likely "effectual" in some cases, but thought it relied too much on women knowing how to insert it correctly, with the possibility that it might become dislodged during intercourse. Concerns about displacement of the womb veil, as well as irritation and loss of pleasurable sensation, were also expressed by the author of an early 20th-century book on human sexuality. The element of unreliability was recognized in the literature distributed by Emma Goldman.

Concerns about fit were addressed by offering over-the-counter womb veils labeled by size, though not in a standardized way: "big" and "small," "one-size-fits-all," and "mothers' size" were some of the terms used. Symptoms such as cramping, abdominal pain, ulceration, and urinary tract infections were likely to have been caused by a too-large womb veil. The risk of dispacement and consequent pregnancy was increased by a veil too small. By comparison, modern diaphragms require cervical measurement and a prescription from a medical practitioner, and range in size from 50 to 95 millimeters.

Noting that "any preventive will fail if not applied properly," the New York physician and free-love advocate Oscar Rotter offered these instructions:

> For introduction, the woman is to sit down, so to say, on her heels, with her legs spread apart, which will bring the womb down as low as possible. Then taking the womb veil into the right hand with the cavity looking upward and compressed from side to side, giving it thus the shape of an ellipse, she has to push it up the vagina as far as it will go. It will then spread out of its own accord and apply itself closely and firmly to the neck of the womb.

Rotter also recommended that the veil be used in conjunction with a spermicide ointment made from muriate of quinine and vaseline. Instructions for removal and hygiene followed.

Rotter was an enthusiastic if careful proponent of the womb veil. Writing in 1897, he recommended pessaries made in England as of the highest quality, with those from Germany also satisfactory. The American in his view were the most poorly made, an inferiority he blamed on the restrictive Comstock laws that drove manufacture and sale underground: "In England, however, where such goods are openly advertised and sold, competition tends to secure the survival of the fittest, and hence it is better to import them from that country." Until legal prohibitions limiting commercial production and distribution were lessened in the 1920s, reputable companies would manufacture devices for contraception only as a discreet sideline. Small-scale entrepreneurs, not excluding black marketeers, stepped in to produce womb veils among other taboo items intended if not explicitly labeled as birth control. For women too poor to buy quality contraception, Rotter also described how to make a homemade device from a rubber ball.

Moral and racialist aspects

The Comstock ban on advertising contraceptive devices, which included womb veils, was not intended to protect consumers from false claims of efficacy, but from exposure to indecency. One editorial writer specifically asserted that even if the ads made true statements, the "anger and indignation of respectable people" at finding such products in their daily newspaper would be grounds to ban them. At Foote's trial, Anthony Comstock himself testified that the womb veil was "an instrument of death both moral and physical to the youth of the land."

The use of womb veils, like other forms of contraception, was thus subject to moral condemnation. In his *Ladies' Guide in Health and Disease*, John Harvey Kellogg asserted several legitimate reasons for family planning, but considered womb veils and other technological forms of birth control to be harmful both physically and psychologically, causing women to lose "all respect for the sacredness of the maternal function." The author of a *Hand-book to Obstetrics* (1908) opined:

> I think there is a growing distaste for the family duties among women ... that should be condemned. The efforts of women to equal man in studies, work, etc., while still claiming their sex privileges, with the dissolution of club and society life, are leading to a 'race suicide.' This ought not to be. Woman is anatomically, physiologically, and emotionally evolved for one sole and single purpose, any departure therefrom being done at the violation of her best ideals and a misdirection of energy.

The author finds the rhythm method ineffective, since "for the female, rut and menstruation are the same." He further disapproves of withdrawal, warning that the latter would lead to "nervous collapse" and noting that "it is infinitely worse than masturbation." The perceived immorality of contraceptive devices was linked to the fear that they might enhance sexual pleasure; like masturbation, the use of womb veils, condoms, and other appliances might "heighten the feeling," but "there is no contact of the parts, and it is morally pernicious and degrading." Because these devices removed the fear of conception, they were said to foster a "positive invitation to illicit intercourse." Although in general douching was more acceptable, even ads for "syringes" could be condemned as being "as hurtful to public morals and children's education as if they advertised condoms and womb veils."

Although birth control was sometimes advocated as a way for the poor to manage their resources better by limiting the size of their family, it could also be promoted for controlling social groups seen as inferior. Observing that a couple "swept away by passion" might not think to take precautions such as inserting a womb veil, and that "the least intelligent" such as "the rough workman or dull peasant" would be most likely not to exercise self-control, one medical writer advocated intrauterine devices that could be left in place "if we wish to breed up not down."

Anxieties about "race suicide" also framed opposition to birth control. The average number of births among white married couples is estimated to have dropped by nearly half between 1800 and 1900. Womb veils were pointed to in racially charged rhetoric warning that contraception threatened the white, specifically Anglo-Saxon, fertility rate. A Missouri physician blamed gynecology as a medical specialty for teaching "young ladies how to avoid conception," claiming that "syringes, sponges, and womb-veils will exterminate the descendants of the Mayflower." An editorial in a 1906 issue of *Texas Medical Journal* asserted that if all physicians were "both civic and Christian gentlemen"

> we should have no criminal abortion cases, no womb veils, no tubes with buttons to close the os, and the Anglo-Saxon race, instead of being in a decadent condition, would rise in its birth rate and not leave the race problem to the Latin-Teutonic and colored race.

In fact, indications are that black Americans also practiced family planning to a comparable degree in the post-slavery period, and several factors seem to have influenced a desire for smaller families among various demographic groups in the 19th century.

See also

- History of condoms
- Timeline of reproductive rights legislation
- Sexuality of Abraham Lincoln, section on Mary Todd Lincoln

Article Sources and Contributors

Diaphragm (contraceptive) *Source*: http://en.wikipedia.org/?oldid=386510667 *Contributors*:

Cervical cap *Source*: http://en.wikipedia.org/?oldid=390630086 *Contributors*: Hmains

Barrier contraception *Source*: http://en.wikipedia.org/?oldid=306541826 *Contributors*: Jamesofur

Contraceptive sponge *Source*: http://en.wikipedia.org/?oldid=387691181 *Contributors*:

Female condom *Source*: http://en.wikipedia.org/?oldid=390042633 *Contributors*: RDBrown

SILCS diaphragm *Source*: http://en.wikipedia.org/?oldid=304501385 *Contributors*: SpaceFlight89

FemCap *Source*: http://en.wikipedia.org/?oldid=370322455 *Contributors*: RDO Medical

Today sponge *Source*: http://en.wikipedia.org/?oldid=378573558 *Contributors*: 1 anonymous edits

Womb veil *Source*: http://en.wikipedia.org/?oldid=370397208 *Contributors*: Eekerz

Image Sources, Licenses and Contributors

Image:Cape cervicale.jpg *Source*: http://en.wikipedia.org/w/index.php?title=File:Cape_cervicale.jpg *License*: unknown *Contributors*: -

Image:Contraception cape cervicale.jpg *Source*: http://en.wikipedia.org/w/index.php?title=File:Contraception_cape_cervicale.jpg *License*: unknown *Contributors*: -

File:Emma Goldman seated.jpg *Source*: http://en.wikipedia.org/w/index.php?title=File:Emma_Goldman_seated.jpg *License*: unknown *Contributors*: -

CPSIA information can be obtained at www.ICGtesting.com
Printed in the USA
LVOW051810291112

309390LV00006B/595/P

9 781242 97253